At the Farm

CR RD CJ AK EM BK DG

Published by The Child's World®, Inc.

Design and Production:
The Creative Spark, San Juan Capistrano, CA

Photos: © 1998 David M. Budd Photography
        pp. 21, 23 © 1999 Equine Photography by Suzanne
Illustrations: Robert Court

Library of Congress Cataloging-in-Publication Data
Francis, Sandy.
    At the farm / by Sandy Francis.
        p. cm.
    Summary. Explains what a farm is, what happens there, who works there,
and the various items and animals that can be found there.
    ISBN 1-56766-574-8 (lib. bdg.: alk. paper)
    1. Agriculture Juvenile literature. 2. Family farms Juvenile literature.
[1. Farms. 2. Farm life.] I. Title.
S519.F726 1999
630—dc21
                                                        99-20225
                                                          CIP

At the
Farm

Written by Sandy Francis
Photos by David M. Budd

F I E L D   T R I P S

The Child's World®, Inc.

Let's go to the farm!

Farms have lots of animals.

Each animal has a job to do.

Dairy cows and goats produce milk.

Cattle, **hogs,** chickens, and sheep provide meat and other **products.**

Farmers also grow **grain** and vegetables.

5

The **farmer** is the person who runs the farm.

His day starts very early.

The rooster gives him a wake-up call.

It crows when the sun comes up

in the morning. Cock-A-Doodle-Doo!

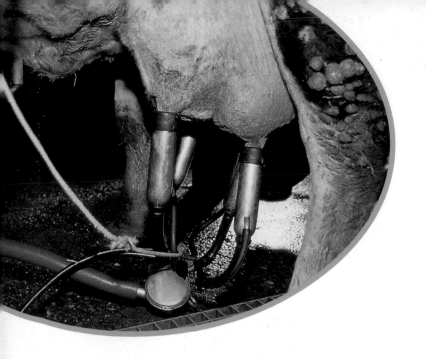

After a good breakfast, the farmer milks
and feeds the dairy cows.
He milks the cows with a machine.
It pumps the milk from the cow into a big tank.
Swoosh! Swoosh!

Some farmers have dairy goats.
They are smaller and easier
to handle than cows.
Goat's milk is used to make
cheese and yogurt.

Goats make good playmates,
too! They like to run and jump.

Lots of baby animals live on a farm.

A baby cow is called a **calf.**

A calf needs milk to grow big and strong.

A baby goat is called a **kid.**

The farmer feeds the babies milk with a bottle.

When they get a little older, he feeds them with a special bucket.

Sometimes the calves and kids kick the buckets and splash the farmer with milk!

Pigs also live on a farm. They eat corn, milk, and leftover vegetables from the garden. The large pigs are called hogs. Hogs provide us with ham, bacon, and other meats.

Hogs like to lay in the mud because it keeps them cool.

This farmer keeps a **flock** of sheep.

Sheep provide many products.

They are raised for **wool** and meat.

Sometimes they are raised for their milk, too.

The sheep's thick wool is cut once or twice

a year. It grows back very quickly.

Wool is used to make clothing, blankets, and many other useful things.

Farmers raise chickens for their eggs and meat.

A **hen** is a female chicken.

She sits on her nest until she lays an egg.

Bok! Bok! Bok!

A baby chicken is called a **chick.**

Peep! Peep! Peep!

The farmer collects the eggs. He sells them to the grocery store.

Horses are also important farm animals.
Long ago, they pulled machines to
plow the fields.
People used horses to get from
place to place, too.
Horses carried people on their backs
or pulled them in carriages.

21

Today most people ride horses for fun.
You can still see big farm horses
at parades or fairs.

This young girl is riding
Western style.

It takes a lot of food to feed
all the farm animals.
Where does the food come from?
Many farmers grow **hay** to feed their animals.
Sometimes farmers grow corn and
other grains, too.
Some farmers buy animal food from
a grain store.

24

Farmers have many jobs to do.

They plow the fields with big machines.

They clean the barns.

They fix the fences and farm machines.

They care for the animals.

A farmer must know how to do many things.

There are so many things to do on a farm!

The farmer often hires helpers.

They help him milk and feed the animals.

They also work in the fields to tend the **crops.**

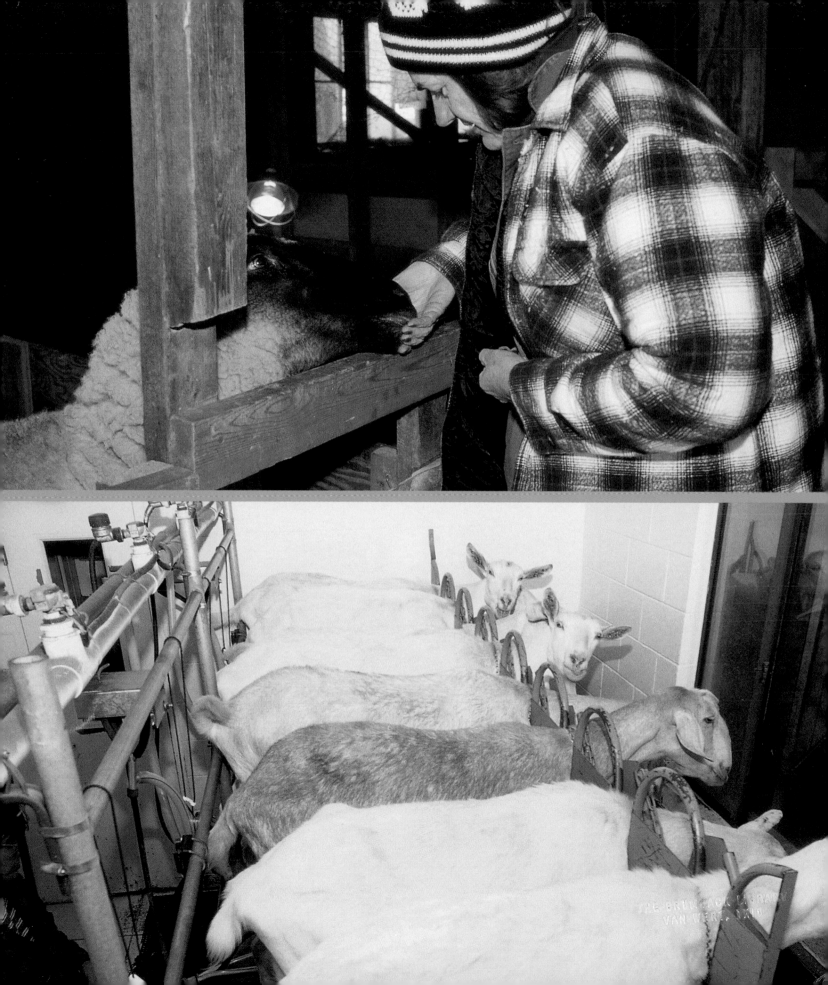

Sometimes the farmers' children raise
special animals to show at fairs.
If they do a good job, they may win a prize!

Farming is a very big job.
Would you like to be a farmer?

Glossary

calf (KAF) — A calf is a baby cow. A calf needs milk to grow big and strong.

chick (CHIK) — A chick is a baby chicken. Chicks hatch from eggs.

crops (KROPZ) — Crops are plants that are grown to produce food. Farmers grow crops to sell to stores or to feed their animals.

dairy (DARE-ee) — A dairy is a farm where animals produce milk. Cows' milk comes from a dairy farm.

farmer (FAR-mer) — A farmer is a person who runs a farm. A farmer has many jobs to do.

flock (FLOK) — A flock is a group of animals. Some farmers have flocks of sheep.

grain (GRANE) — Grain is food that comes from the seeds of grassy plants. Grain provides food for people and animals.

hay (HAY) — Hay is a kind of grass that farmers grow. Hay is used to feed many farm animals.

hen (HEN) — A hen is a female chicken. A hen lays eggs.

hogs (HOGZ) — Hogs are male pigs. Ham, bacon, and many other products come from hogs.

kid (KID) — A kid is a baby goat. Farmers sometimes feed kids with baby bottles.

plow (PLAU) — When farmers plow the soil, they move it around and break it up. Farmers plow the farm's fields.

products (PRAW-duktz) — Products are things that farmers grow to use or sell. Milk is a dairy product.

wool (WOOHL) — Wool is the soft hair that covers sheep. Wool is used to make clothing and blankets.

Index

32

Sandy Francis lives in upstate New York with her husband, son, and dog, Barklee. She enjoys gardening and writing children's stories inspired by the creative spirit of her grandchildren.